Casey's Cocktails

Nathan Cameron
Casey's Mixologist

Photography by Brian MacDonald

Casey's
grill • bar

DINE *and* **DISCOVER**

First published in Canada in 2007
by Prime Restaurants of Canada Inc.
10 Kingsbridge Garden Circle, Suite 600
Mississauga, Ontario L5R 3K6
www.primerestaurants.com
www.caseysbarandgrill.com

ISBN 978-0-9784230-0-1

10   9   8   7   6   5   4   3   2   1

Printed in Canada

Contents

Introduction

When Casey's opened its doors in Sudbury, Ontario, in 1980, we served our first Bloody Caesar. It was an instant classic. Thirty years later and everything has changed — except the original recipe for the Casey's Classic Caesar. A cocktail is no longer simply a drink, but a creation dreamed up not by a bartender, but a mixoligist. Standards such as a rye and Coke, a screwdriver, or even a gin and tonic have been marginalized as "traditional" cocktails, enjoyed by adults of a certain age. No longer content to be relegated to the opening act, cocktails have taken centre stage. Their very names — Sex in the City, Madagascar Margarita, and Chocolate Addiction — hint of sensuous and seductive flavours and experiences. A cocktail is a mix of inspiration, creativity and the latest and freshest ingredients. The cocktail is culture now — synthesized and poured all into an eight-ounce glass.

Get ready to start pouring, crushing, mixing, slicing and straining. Step by step, from the essential tools, glassware and ingredients, to preparation techniques and tricks of the trade, everything you need to create and enjoy Casey's famous cocktails awaits your discovery. Twenty-four recipes including Casey's Classic Caesar, martinis brimming with fresh fruit flavours — a blueberry or perhaps a lychee martini, anyone? — and even cocktails for dessert, all leave your guests thirsty for more.

Cocktail Basics

You don't need to be a professional bartender to create the perfect cocktail. But you do need to remember four essential elements that will make every one of your creations — from presentation to taste — memorable from the first sip to the bottom of the glass. The first and most important rule is to use the best and freshest ingredients available; second, use the proper mixing tools; third, employ the correct mixing technique; and finally, consider the presentation — the right glasses and garnishes will create a memorable first impression.

Cocktail Tools

For the perfect cocktail, start with the correct tools. Not only will your creations taste great, but the process will be easier and the experience more fun.

BOSTON SHAKER — The Boston shaker is the shaker preferred by most bartenders as it allows you to watch the cocktail as it mixes. The Boston shaker has two parts: a glass sleeve, which fits snugly into a larger metal container or shell, and a Hawthorne strainer, which is used along with the shaker. The Hawthorne strainer has springs allowing for easy pouring control with a mixing glass or shaker.

MUDDLING STICK — A muddling stick, the cocktail equivalent of a pestle, is used to crush fruit, sugar cubes, herbs or mint to release their flavours and juices. The muddling is usually done in the cocktail shaker or in the cocktail glass itself.

BAR SPOON — It's all about size, as a bar spoon of sufficient length allows for stirring at the bottom of a long cocktail. The best bar spoons have a twisted stem and a flat bottom for control.

10 oz
9 oz
8 oz
7 oz
6 oz
5 oz
4 oz
3 oz
2 oz

MEASURING DEVICE — Jiggers are measuring "thimbles" that usually come in measures equal to 1 US fluid ounce (30 ml), 1½ ounces (45 ml), and 2 fluid ounces (60 ml). Jiggers make easy work of measuring spirits or mixes precisely. A standard 1-ounce shot glass would be a secondary option.

BLENDER — Indispensable for blended cocktails, but use only crushed ice; ice cubes can damage the blender's blades. Pour the liquid ingredients in first and then add the ice, so the ice doesn't melt before mixing. Begin on the slowest setting and build up to the fastest.

ZESTER — The zest of citrus fruit, particularly lemon, lime and orange, is used to flavour certain cocktails. Take care to zest only the skin and not the plinth, which can be bitter.

Mixing Techniques

SHAKING — Shaking cocktails can be fun for you and your guests. Fill a cocktail shaker with ice cubes before adding the desired ingredients. Shake up and down for about 10 seconds. Remember to hold both the shaker and the Boston glass firmly to avoid spillage. Place a Hawthorne strainer over the Boston glass and strain into the desired glass. When straining muddled fruit or dense purées hold the Hawthorne strainer loosely in place to allow the fruit or mix to pass through into the cocktail or martini.

STIRRING — This method is used when you do not want to disturb the texture of a particular juice, such as when making a Casey's Classic Caesar. Stirring allows you to mix the ingredients without violently smashing the ingredients together.

BLENDING — Using a blender, ice and the cocktail ingredients are combined and blended until smooth.

BUILDING — The simplest method of creating a cocktail. The ingredients are measured, poured over ice and given a quick stir according to the recipe.

PRESENTATION & GARNISHES — As in all culinary creations, an attractive fresh garnish can make the difference between a good cocktail and a memorable one. There are no hard and fast rules — you are limited only by your imagination. The key is to always use the freshest ingredients you can find. When it comes to the presentation, think colour and freshness. Wait until the last possible moment to prepare your desired garnishes for a picture-perfect drink.

GLASS RIMMING — Cut a thick wedge of lime and gently and evenly rub it around the rim of the glass. Now roll the outer rim of the glass over a saucer of salt, sugar or desired ingredients according to the recipe. Last, take the lime and run it around the inside of the glass to remove any stray crystals that might fall into the drink.

Bar 101 at Home

A well-stocked bar will give you the basics to create a variety of traditional and innovative cocktails. Let's begin with the essential base spirits.

SMIRNOFF® VODKA — Voted the the Number 1 and Best Tasting Vodka by the *New York Times* in 2005, *Smirnoff Vodka* is distinguished by its perfectly balanced character. Crafted from the finest grains, *Smirnoff Vodka* is triple distilled and ten times filtered through birch tree charcoal for exceptional purity and a clean, smooth taste.

TANQUERAY ®GIN — Made from the top 10 percent of the finest botanicals for the distillation process and quadruple distilled, *Tanqueray* has a rich juniper flavour and is used in cocktails such as the T&T (*Tanqueray* and tonic) and features as the main ingredient in a memorable martini.

JOSE CUERVO® GOLD TEQUILA — The Number 1 tequila in the world is a well-balanced, slightly sweet tequila with subtle flavours of agave, vanilla and oak. A premium tequila, *Jose Cuervo Gold* will take a frozen or shaken margarita to the next level.

CAPTAIN MORGAN® WHITE RUM — This classic white rum evokes images of sun-drenched beaches, Caribbean Islands and Sir Captain Henry Morgan, who is known to have sparked some legendary times most frequently with cola, orange juice and a variety of fruit juices.

CROWN ROYAL® CANADIAN WHISKY — This full-bodied blend of distinctive whiskies is matured to perfection to create refined richness, robust flavour and smoothness enhanced by a rich, lingering finish.

Flavouring Agents

You can concoct your own or choose from a variety of ready-made flavouring agents to enhance and highlight the characteristics of your chosen base spirit.

FLAVOURED SPIRITS — There are endless options when it comes to flavoured spirits. Adding a small amount of a flavoured spirit to a base spirit can bring balance and enhance the overall taste profile of a cocktail.

SIMPLE SYRUP — In a small saucepan, combine 1 cup (8 oz./250 ml) water with 1 cup (8 oz./250 g) sugar. Bring to a boil over medium heat, stirring until sugar dissolves. Remove from heat and let stand to cool. Pour into a bottle, seal and store in the refrigerator.

FRUIT PURÉES — There are many commercial fruit purées available at local grocery and specialty stores. An even better alternative is making your own. Put a small amount of the desired fruit in a food processor or blender with a tablespoon of simple syrup. Blend until smooth and use as required.

SYRUPS — Commercial syrups can add flavour and complexity to a drink. There are wide ranges of domestic and exotic flavours available in many grocery stores.

Strawberry Lychee Martini

The lychee fruit is also known as the "Chinese cherry." The lychee tree can measure up to 20 to 30 meters high. The fruit grows in bunches and telescopic fruit gatherers are needed to reach them.

Ingredients

1½ oz. *Smirnoff* vodka

½ oz. *Soho* lychee liqueur

2 whole strawberries

3 oz. white cranberry juice

¼ oz. simple syrup

1 lychee, for garnish

Method

Muddle well two fresh strawberries with the stems removed. Add vodka, lychee liqueur, simple syrup and white cranberry juice to a cocktail shaker. Add ice and shake vigorously, then loosely strain into a chilled martini glass.

Garnish

Skewer a whole lychee fruit and place in the martini glass.

Blueberry Frost

Ingredients

2 oz. *Parrot Bay* coconut rum

2 oz. blueberry purée

3 oz. pineapple juice

fresh blueberries, for garnish

Method

Half fill a cocktail shaker with ice. Add coconut rum, blueberry purée and pineapple juice. Shake well and strain into a chilled martini glass.

Garnish

Skewer three fresh blueberries and place across the top of the martini glass.

THE POWER OF BLUE
Blueberries are loaded with anti-aging dietary antioxidants that are said to prevent heart disease, some forms of cancer, and help restore memory and vision.

Cabo Cosmo

The greatness is all in the balance. Temper a spirit with a strong, perhaps even bitter profile (*Jose Cuervo Gold Especial* tequila) with a very sweet spirit (*Navan*) to produce a well-balanced final product.

Ingredients

1 oz. *Jose Cuervo Gold Especial* tequila

½ oz. *Navan* — a Madagascar vanilla-infused cognac

2 oz. white cranberry juice

¼ wedge fresh lime

lime slices, for garnish

Method

Half fill a cocktail shaker with ice. Add tequila, *Navan* and white cranberry juice, then squeeze a ¼ wedge of lime over the liquid and drop the wedge itself in the cocktail shaker. Shake well and strain into a chilled martini glass.

Garnish

Add two or three thin slices of fresh lime to the glass to give this martini additional flavour and balance the taste profile.

Chocolate Addiction

CHOCOLATE ADDICTION
Italian researchers have reported that chocolate can have a positive physiological impact on a woman's sexuality. Need we say more? Drink up!

Ingredients

1 oz. *Baileys Mint Chocolate Irish Cream*
½ oz. crème de cacao – chocolate liqueur
2 oz. chilled mocha espresso
1 oz. white 2-percent milk
chocolate sauce, grated chocolate, for garnish

Method

Half fill a cocktail shaker with ice. Add *Baileys Mint Chocolate Irish Cream*, chocolate liqueur, espresso and a splash of milk. Shake vigorously and strain into a chocolate-rimmed chilled cocktail glass. When straining into the glass, hold the shaker well above to create a nice froth on the top of this cocktail.

Garnish

Fill a shallow side plate with chocolate sauce. Dip the rim of the cocktail glass in the chocolate sauce, then refrigerate to harden. When ready to serve, using a grater, shave more chocolate on top of the froth.

Tango

Ingredients

1 oz. *Captain Morgan* dark rum

½ oz. *Archer's* peach schnapps

3 oz. passion fruit juice

1 oz. guava juice

star fruit slice, for garnish

Method

Half fill a cocktail shaker with ice. Add rum, peach schnapps, passion fruit juice and guava juice. Shake well and strain into a chilled martini glass.

Garnish

Place a thin slice of star fruit on the rim of the martini glass.

DRINKING LEADS TO DANCE

The tango is a social dance originating in Buenos Aires, Argentina. Naturally we wanted South and Central American fruit to pair well for the dance. Passion fruit and guava make perfect dance partners when combined with the distinctive rich and smooth experience of *Captain Morgan* dark rum.

Peppered Berry

STRAWBERRIES

Strawberries are among the most versatile of all the fresh fruits when it comes to mixing cocktails. Unfortunately, they are also quite perishable. Strawberries work very well with most of the base spirits, including gin, rum, tequila and vodka.

Ingredients

¾ oz. *Smirnoff Strawberry* vodka

¾ oz. *Navan* — a Madagascar vanilla-infused cognac

2 oz. white cranberry juice

1 grind of fresh ground pepper

pepper-dusted strawberry, for garnish

Method

Half fill a cocktail shaker with ice. Add vodka, *Navan*, white cranberry juice and a pinch of fresh ground black pepper. Shake well and strain into a chilled martini glass.

Garnish

Using a pepper mill, grind one rotation on the surface of the martini. Place a pepper-dusted strawberry on the rim of the martini glass.

Sex in the City

Ingredients

1 oz. *Smirnoff* vodka

1 oz. *Sour Puss* raspberry liqueur

6 fresh raspberries

3 oz. cranberry juice

raspberry rock candy, lime wedge, raspberries, for garnish

SEX IN THE CITY

Named after the TV show, this glam cocktail boosts its wow factor with a raspberry rim. As a first-date drink, it is sure to please — and may lead to that oh-so-innocent question, "Is there any alcohol in this?"

Method

Muddle fresh raspberries along with vodka and sour raspberry liqueur in a cocktail shaker. Half fill the cocktail shaker with ice and add cranberry juice. Shake well and strain into a rock-candy-rimmed chilled martini glass.

Garnish

Place raspberry rock candy on a shallow plate. Gently rub the rim of the martini glass with the lime wedge then dip in a shallow plate of crushed raspberry rock candy. Garnish with two fresh raspberries.

Green Apple Crush

GREEN APPLES

There are more than 7,000 varieties of apples. Its antioxidant agents have earned the fruit the old saying, "An apple a day keeps the drink doctor employed."

Ingredients

1 oz. *Smirnoff Green Apple* vodka

½ oz. *Cointreau* — premium orange liqueur

4 oz. cranberry juice

¼ green apple

green apple slices, fresh mint, for garnish

Method

Half fill a cocktail shaker with ice. Add vodka, *Cointreau* and cranberry juice. Shake well and strain over an ice-packed cocktail glass with green apple pieces.

Garnish

Cut a green apple into thin slices and add to the ice in each glass as desired. Finish with a fresh mint sprig.

Vanilla Pom

POMEGRANATE grows in regions from Iran to the Himalayas in northern India, and has been cultivated and naturalized throughout the Mediterranean since ancient times. Pomegranate juice contains high levels of antioxidants — higher than most other fruit juices, red wine or green tea.

Ingredients

1½ oz. *Smirnoff Vanilla* vodka

½ oz. cassis – black currant liqueur

2 oz. pomegranate juice

2 oz. pineapple juice

blackberries, for garnish

Method

Half fill a cocktail shaker with ice. Add vodka, cassis, pomegranate and pineapple juices. Shake well and strain over an ice-packed cocktail glass.

Garnish

Skewer two fresh blackberries and place across the top of the cocktail glass.

South Beach

Ingredients

1 oz. *Parrot Bay* coconut rum

1 oz. *Hpnotiq* — fruit-infused cognac

3 oz. pineapple juice

2 shakes of cinnamon powder

pineapple wedges, cinnamon powder, for garnish

Method

Half fill a cocktail shaker with ice. Add coconut rum, *Hpnotiq*, pineapple juice and cinnamon. Shake well and strain into a chilled martini glass.

Garnish

Slice a fresh pineapple into discs, then cut into triangular pieces. Cut into the tip of a wedge and place on the rim of the martini glass. Lightly dust the froth of the martini with cinnamon.

SPICED UP

Adding spices can really enhance a drink's taste profile. This drink marries *Parrot Bay*'s sweet coconut taste with pineapple, cinnamon and the tropical fruits used in *Hpnotiq*. The result is a slightly sweet, fruity, and complex drink that makes you look like a pro.

Perfect "10"

THE MARTINI

This is possibly the most famous and sophisticated cocktail ever mixed. There are stories about its exact origins, but many believe that it was first made in 1911 at New York's Knickerbocker Hotel by a bartender named Martini.

Ingredients

2 oz. *Tanqueray No. Ten* gin
Martini Rosso extra-dry vermouth
lemon twist or vermouth-spiked colossal
stuffed olives, for garnish

Method

Place a very small amount of room-temperature vermouth in a chilled martini glass. Swirl the vermouth around the glass, making sure to coat as much of the glass as possible. Dump any excess. Half fill a cocktail shaker with ice and add the gin. Shake well and strain into the chilled, vermouth-rinsed martini glass.

Garnish

Depending on your preference, place either a lemon twist or a skewer of vermouth-spiked colossal stuffed olives into the martini.

Lychee Berry

Ingredients

1¼ oz. *Tanqueray* gin

¼ oz. *Soho* lychee liqueur

2 whole strawberries

½ kiwi fruit

3 oz. cranberry juice

kiwi fruit, for garnish

Method

Place two strawberries and half a peeled kiwi cut into pieces into a cocktail shaker. Add gin and lychee liqueur. Muddle fruit until desired consistency. Half fill the cocktail shaker with ice and add cranberry juice. Shake well and loosely strain over an ice-packed cocktail glass.

Garnish

Cut a disc from the other half of the kiwi and place on the rim of the cocktail glass.

THE CLASSIC

Tanqueray, the classic gin recipe developed in 1830, has earned double gold in each of the last four years at the San Francisco World Spirit Championships. *Tanqueray* has a complex and smooth finish with flavours of orange, lime and fresh juniper berries.

Ultimate Margarita

Ingredients

1 oz. *Jose Cuervo Gold* tequila
½ oz. *Grand Marnier*
3 oz. *Jose Cuervo* margarita mix
1 oz. fresh lime juice
¼ oz. simple syrup
sea salt, lime wedge, for garnish

Method

Half fill a cocktail shaker with ice. Add tequila, *Grand Marnier*, margarita mix, lime juice and simple syrup. Shake well and strain over an ice-filled, sea-salt-rimmed margarita glass.

Garnish

Gently rub the rim of the margarita glass with the wedge of lime then dip the rim in a shallow plate of sea salt. Place a lime wedge on the rim of the margarita glass.

DID YOU KNOW

There are four types of tequila:

1. White/Silver or Blanco/Plata — No aging is required. A maximum of 30 days in a barrel. Best served straight up or on the rocks.

2. Gold or Oro/Joven — Any aged tequila which has been blended with even a small amount of white tequila. Best served as shots and in the perfect *Jose Cuervo Gold* margarita.

3. Rested or Resposado — Rested between two and twelve months in oak. Makes the best premium *Jose Cuervo* margarita. Excellent as a chilled shot or served straight for sipping.

4. Aged or Anejo — Rested in small oak barrels for a minimum of one year.

Madagascar Margarita

MADAGASCAR VANILLA

Today vanilla beans are grown in four major areas of the world, each with distinctive characteristics and attributes. Madagascar, an island off the coast of Africa, is the largest producer of vanilla beans in the world and their vanilla is known as Madagascar Bourbon vanilla. The term Bourbon applies to the beans grown on the Bourbon islands — Madagascar, Comoro, Seychelle and Reunion. Madagascar Bourbon Vanilla is considered the highest quality pure vanilla available.

Ingredients

1 oz. *Jose Cuervo Classico* tequila

½ oz. *Navan* — a Madagascar vanilla-infused cognac

3 oz. *Jose Cuervo* margarita mix

1 oz. fresh lime juice

vanilla beans, fresh mint, for garnish

Method

Half fill a cocktail shaker with ice. Add tequila, *Navan*, margarita mix and lime juice. Shake well and strain over an ice-packed margarita glass.

Garnish

Place two vanilla beans in the glass — not only will they add a great visual but they will increase the vanilla profile. Finish with a fresh mint sprig.

Passion Fruit Margarita

Ingredients

1 oz. *Jose Cuervo Especial Gold* tequila

½ oz. *Cointreau*

2 oz. passion fruit juice

1 oz. *Jose Cuervo* margarita mix

1 oz. fresh lime juice

green apple, pineapple leaves, for garnish

Method

Half fill a cocktail shaker with ice. Add tequila, *Cointreau*, margarita mix, passion fruit and lime juices. Shake well and strain over an ice-packed margarita glass.

Garnish

Arrange a wedge of green apple and two pineapple leaves in one side of the margarita glass.

CINCO DE MAYO

"The Fifth of May" is a national holiday in Mexico, also widely celebrated in the United States. It commemorates the victory of Mexican forces led by General Ignacio Zaragoza over the French occupational forces in the Battle of Puebla on May 5, 1862. And it makes a good excuse to drink some tequila.

Frozen Caramel Macchiato

Ingredients

2 oz. *Baileys Caramel Irish Cream*

1 oz. mocha cappuccino

3 oz. French vanilla yogurt

1 oz. 2-percent white milk

caramel sauce, caramel wafer, for garnish

Method

Add all ingredients along with a large scoop
of crushed ice to a blender. Blend until it reaches
the desired texture and pour into a cocktail glass.

Garnish

Using a squeeze bottle of caramel, spiral caramel
around the inside of a cocktail glass. Add a
caramel swirl on the top and a caramel wafer in one
side of the blended cocktail.

COFFEE COCKTAILS

When we think of coffee and liquor,
the first drink that comes to mind is
usually Irish coffee, a 1940s
creation of Joe Sheridan, a
bartender at Shannon Airport,
Ireland. The tradition apparently
began with sambuca, an Italian
anise-flavoured liqueur often served
alongside a cup of espresso as a
post-meal potion. Now bartenders
everywhere offer their own
signature creations made with
espresso, cappuccino and other
coffee concoctions.

Wild Berry Caprioska

DESSERT OR DRINK?

This cocktail is a drink that could almost be served as a dessert. A vodka version of the Brazilian classic caipirinha, it is like a sangria in the amount of fruit it contains. You can vary the fruits and the amount of vodka to please your own taste. It's hard to serve with a straw because the fruit gets in the way. You may want to consider a spoon with this one.

Ingredients

1½ oz. *Smirnoff* vodka

3 tbsp. fresh berries

⅛ lime wedge

¼ oz. simple syrup

fresh blueberry, raspberry, blackberry, for garnish

Method

Squeeze lime wedge and drop into a cocktail shaker along with wild berries and simple syrup. Muddle berries well. Half fill the cocktail shaker with ice and add vodka. Shake vigorously and strain over an ice-packed cocktail glass.

Garnish

Add one fresh blueberry, raspberry and blackberry to a skewer and place across the top of the cocktail glass.

Mandarin Mojito

Ingredients

1½ oz. *Captain Morgan* white rum

6 small wedges of Mandarin orange

8 fresh mint leaves

3 lime wedges

¼ oz. simple syrup

3 oz. passion fruit juice

1 oz. soda

fresh mint, for garnish

Method

Add rum, Mandarin oranges, mint, lime and simple syrup to a cocktail glass. Muddle well. Fill the glass with ice cubes. Pour passion fruit juice over the ice. Stir well and top with a splash of soda.

Garnish

Top the Mojito with a sprig of fresh mint.

MOJITO, A PIRATE'S DRINK?
It was English pirate Richard Drake who prepared the first version of the Mojito, originally named "El Draque" (or the Dragon, after his boss Sir Francis). Story has it that swashbucklers on treasure-hunting escapades through the Caribbean and Latin America first introduced the Mojito to Cuba.

Mister Tea

Ingredients

1½ oz. *Captain Morgan* spiced rum

½ oz. pomegranate liqueur

2 oz. cranberry juice

1 oz. iced tea

blueberries, for garnish

Method

Half fill a cocktail shaker with ice. Add all ingredients except blueberries to a cocktail shaker. Shake well and strain over an ice-packed cocktail glass with fresh blueberries.

Garnish

Arrange fresh blueberries throughout the ice in the cocktail glass.

SPICED RUM

Contrary to popular belief, *Captain Morgan* spiced rum is not spicy and acts more as a complement to other flavours. It marries well with colas especially because of its prominent vanilla flavours and the hint of fruit makes it a good match for juices such as cranberry and orange.

Raspberry Crush

Ingredients

1½ oz. *Smirnoff Lime* vodka

2 wedges of fresh lime

6 fresh raspberries

2 oz. pineapple juice

raspberries, lime, for garnish

Method

Add fresh raspberries, fresh lime and vodka into a cocktail glass and muddle well. Fill the glass with ice, top with pineapple juice and stir well.

Garnish

Skewer fresh raspberries and lime and place on top of the cocktail.

Casey's Classic Caesar

HAIL CAESAR!

The Caesar was invented in 1969 by mixologist Walter Chenell in Calgary. Chenell named his drink after the Roman emperor. Then he served one to an Englishman who exclaimed, "That's a bloody good Caesar!" A legend was born.

Ingredients

1½ oz. *Smirnoff* vodka

6 oz. *Mott's® Clamato®*

6 dashes worcestershire sauce

4 drops of tabasco sauce

dash of salt and pepper

celery salt

celery stalk, lime wheel and red finger pepper, for garnish

Method

Gently rub the rim of a large goblet with a lime wedge then dip in a shallow plate of celery salt. Fill the celery-salt-rimmed goblet with ice. Add vodka, salt and pepper, tabasco and worcestershire sauces. Top with *Clamato* juice and stir well.

Garnish

Place a freshly cut celery stalk into the Caesar, add a lime wheel on the rim and a red finger pepper across the top of the glass.

Firehouse Caesar

Ingredients

1 oz. *Smirnoff* vodka

4 drops habanero tabasco sauce

2 shakes cayenne pepper

4 drops worcestershire sauce

6 oz. *Mott's Clamato*

dash of salt and pepper

celery stalk, red finger pepper and
Extreme Bean, for garnish

Method

Gently rub the rim of the stemmed cocktail glass with a
lime wedge then dip in a shallow plate of Caesar rim mix.
Fill the Caesar-rim-mixed glass with ice. Add vodka,
tabasco, worcestershire sauce, cayenne pepper and salt
and pepper. Top with *Clamato* juice and stir well.

Garnish

Add a fresh celery stalk, red finger pepper and an *Extreme
Bean* (marinated green bean) to the Caesar.

HABANERO PEPPERS

The hottest known pepper in
the world, habaneros are said
to be 100 times hotter than
jalapeno. Prized by chile
aficionados not only for its
intense heat, but also its
distinctive fruitiness, the
habanero is a great addition to
the Canadian-born classic
cocktail.

Apple Crisp

Ingredients

¾ oz. *Captain Morgan* spiced rum

¾ oz. butterscotch ripple

hot apple cider

brown sugar and powdered cinnamon mix, cinnamon stick, for garnish

Method

Add rum and butterscotch liqueur to a rimmed heatproof specialty coffee glass. Top with hot apple cider.

Garnish

Rim the specialty coffee glass with a baked brown sugar and cinnamon mix. Bake brown sugar in the oven on a baking sheet for approximately 15 minutes at 400°F. Mix together four parts cooled brown sugar to one part powdered cinnamon. Place a cinnamon stick in the heatproof mug.

CAKETAILS

Using a favourite culinary item for inspiration is a great innovative way to deliver something different to your guests. Apple crisp is one of many featured caketails (dessert-inspired cocktails) featured at *Casey's* during the cold winter months.

German Chocolate Cake

Ingredients

½ oz. *Parrot Bay* coconut rum

½ oz. *Godiva* white chocolate liqueur

½ oz. *Frangelico*

5 oz. hot chocolate

whipped cream, grated cinnamon, for garnish

Method

Add coconut rum and liqueurs to a heatproof specialty coffee glass. Top with rich hot chocolate.

Garnish

Top the specialty coffee glass with real whipped cream and grated chocolate.

SPIRIT FLAVOURS

Understanding the flavours behind the various liqueurs is essential when mimicking a culinary item such as a classic dessert. You can then have fun choosing flavouring agents to add your own twist to your cocktail. We chose a coconut rum to replace the coconut frosting, *Frangelico* for the nutty hazelnut flavour and finally, the *Godiva* chocolate liqueur for the rich chocolate cake.

Index

Acknowledgments

Creating a perfect cocktail calls for specific ingredients in exact measure, each imparting their specific characteristics to the whole, some subtly and others more boldly, creating something unexpectedly new and exciting. The following individuals each contributed their own talent and flare to create the unique flavour of *Casey's Cocktails*: Nick Perpick, the founder of Casey's and the COO of Prime Restaurants, who in his time behind the bar, back where it all started in Sudbury in 1980, mixed more than one Casey's Classic Caesar; at Diageo Canada, Peter Kourtis, Tim Kennelly and Debbie Stevens for their tireless championing of *Casey's Cocktails*, and of course, the Diageo brand team including Andrea Sengara, Paul Neuman, Rodolfo Aldana, Roisin Meagher and Winnie Mittal for their enthusiastic support of the project; Ross Bain, for sage legal counsel and an exacting eye for detail; and the entire Casey's team, and their commitment to taste and re-taste the recipes, all in the name of perfection.

Casey's Cocktails was produced for Prime Restaurants of Canada Inc. under the direction of Jack Gardner.
Book design by Gordon Sibley, edited by Kathleen Fraser.

REFRESHING QUALITY...

DIAGEO